1

There were over 250 First People's languages in Australia.

This is some of the languages in Western Australia.

Miriwoong

Bardi

Bunuba   Kija

Gooniyandi   Jaru

Walmajarri

Nyangumarta   Kakatja

Yindjibarndi   Pintupi

Banyjima   Martu Wangka

Pitjantjatjara

Manjiljarra

Ngaanyatjarra

Wangkatha

Noongar

3

The Gibber Desert is in Australia. 'Gibber' is a word by the First People. Gibber means stone.

'Bu-ma-rang' was the name by the Dha-ra-wal people. The name was changed to boomerang. It was used for hunting.

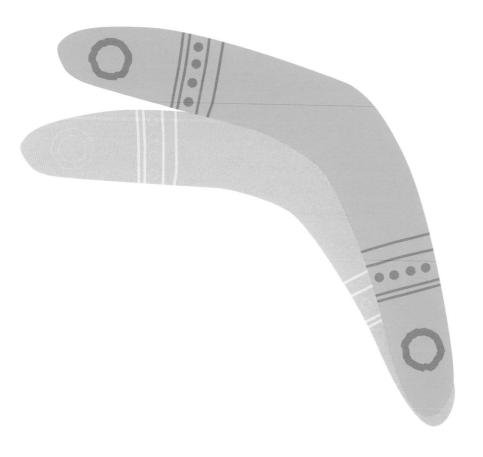

7

Some words were spoken by other tribes. 'Yaba' was to speak.

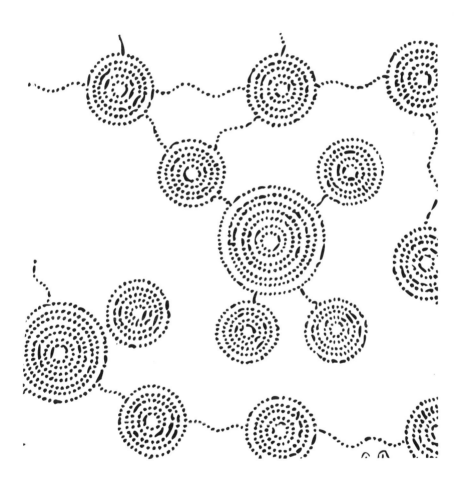

'Cooee' was a word of Southern
NSW First People.

11

'Yakka' meant work for the
Toorbul people of Brisbane.

12

13

'Min-gi' is the Yolnju people's word for 'fire fly'.

15

The Dharuk people called it 'Gu-la'. We call it koala.

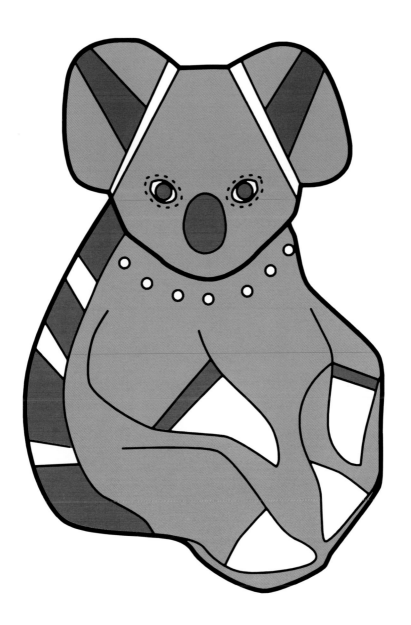

17

The 'Wum-bat' is a First People name for wombat.

19

The snake was 'Ka-bul' to the Toorbul people.

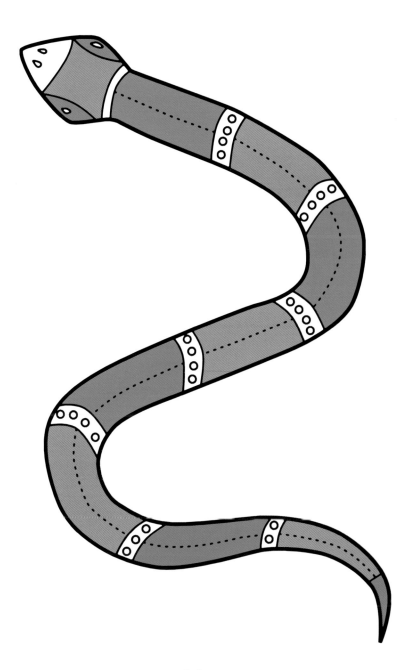

21

'Wa-mu' was a flying fox to First People in Victoria.

23

Word bank

boomerang

Dharawal

spoken

tribes

Victoria

snake

koala

Yolnju

southern

Toorbul

people

Brisbane

wombat